VANISHING

THE
FRASER ISLAND
DINGO

JENNIFER
PARKHURST

GREY THRUSH PUBLISHING

National Library of Australia Cataloguing-in-Publication entry

    Author: Parkhurst, Jennifer.

    Title: Vanishing icon : the Fraser Island dingo / Jennifer Parkhurst.

    ISBN: 9780980743517 (pbk.)

    Subjects: Dingo--Queensland--Fraser Island.

    Endangered species--Queensland--Fraser Island.
    Natural history--Queensland--Fraser Island.
    Fraser Island (Qld.)

    Dewey Number: 599.772099432

Published by **Grey Thrush Publishing**
an imprint of
ORYX PUBLISHING Pty Ltd
13 Marlton Crescent
St Kilda 3182
Printed in Melbourne by OnDemand

Introduction

I met my first dingo over 25 years ago on the beach in Womboyne National Park, New South Wales. It was love at first sight. So began a quest of discovery, a journey that has taken me to almost every state in Australia – through the outback, along little-used desert tracks, to places remote and strange, and, inevitably, to Fraser Island.

Fraser Island or K'Gari (Paradise) is home to the Butchulla people, traditional owners of this land and surrounding areas. They hold the dingo in high esteem and, along with the dolphin, the dingo is a totemic animal on the Island. Over the years, I have spoken at length with many living descendents and various Butchulla elders who have given my work with dingoes their blessing. They have even bestowed on me the special Aboriginal name, 'Naibar Wangari Yeeran', which means 'Our Sister Dingo Woman'.

Dingoes on the Island have always had some sort of human contact both with the indigenous people, and later, with the forestry workers, who fed, wormed, and befriended them. Some even had 'pet' dingoes that whelped their pups under the workers' dongas. Until the fencing went up around the townships, the same relationship occurred between dingoes and township residents. With the massive influx of tourism over the past 10 years, it is impossible for dingoes to avoid people.

Every life matters – even that of an animal that is despised by some, frequently persecuted and needlessly killed, but continues on its own to struggle to survive despite extreme adversity in a world that wishes it did not exist at all.

I hope this book conveys the wonderful character of the dingo and their amazing capacity to show affection and concern for each other. All the photos were taken with a minimum of interference to the animals. I operated on the principle of maintaining a safe distance and waiting to see what might happen. It is almost impossible to hide from a dingo and once they arrived at their secret areas they inevitably knew I was there.

Like all dingoes on Fraser Island the female I called Kirra enjoyed cooling off in the surf.

This bonded pair of young dingoes enjoys a rest in the winter sunshine behind the dunes, completely unconcerned by my presence.

Because I was never afraid of the dingoes and never reacted to them with anything but respect, they were not alarmed by me and went about their normal activities despite my presence. Thus, by sitting still and quietly for up to four hours at times, I was able to observe the most intimate moments of the dingoes' lives.

Trust is earned, not demanded. and I never presumed to demand anything from the dingoes. This was their world and their territory and I was an intruder. There was never an occasion when I felt personally threatened – even by some of the large alpha males who were protecting or parenting their pups.

None of the photos in this book were obtained by luring the dingoes to me with food. Perhaps those people who have accused me of this simply could not understand how I was able to capture such intimate moments without doing so.

So please enjoy these photos taken over a period of years, all taken with respect and love. and with the aim of showing the world what an awesome animal our Australian dingo is.

World Heritage icon

Dingoes have been living on Fraser Island for at least one thousand years – they remain as one of the purest strains of dingo in eastern Australia. Yet fewer than 200 of these magnificent animals remain on the Island – their fate hangs in the balance. For the hundreds of thousands of people who come each year from around the globe to this World Heritage sanctuary, the sighting of a dingo provides a special thrill.

Lithe and mysterious, the dingo appeals to the 'call of the wild' in most of us; its melancholy howl echoing through the undergrowth reminds us that a being exists somewhere close, living a secret life that few of us will ever know about.

As a photographic subject, the dingo is challenging and surprising. Never predictable or easy to pin down, it can evade us in its natural environment as easily as breathing. If the dingo wants you to see it, you will – otherwise, it evaporates into the bush and you would never have known it existed.

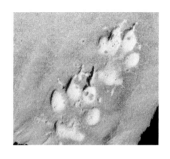

The beaches of Fraser Island give dingoes the opportunity to enjoy a spot of fishing, or forage on a dolphin, dugong or turtle carcass that has washed up onto the shore.

Dingo pups with their oversized ears, inquisitive brown eyes and playful manner inspire us to consider the gentler side of this much-maligned mammal.

Most Australians have a strong opinion about the dingo. Because of the Lindy Chamberlain case in central Australia and one fatal attack on a young child on Fraser Island, the dingo has become infamous. But does it deserve to be condemned or should it command the same respect and admiration enjoyed by top-end predators in other countries around the world, such as the lion, the tiger or the great white shark?

Despite much persecution, dingoes have a long history of coexisting with people while eking out their own meagre living in their ever-shrinking environment.

The dingo and Aboriginal culture

Myth, legend, hypothesis and scientific evidence all combine to unravel the compelling and continuing mystery – how did the dingo first appear in Australia? Most researchers now agree that the dingo was brought to the Australian continent by Asian sea-faring traders some 5000 years ago. Evidence for this comes from dingo fossils and from Aboriginal cave paintings of dingoes from this era. DNA evidence further suggests that all dingoes in Australia may be descended from one single pregnant female!

No one knows for sure how the dingo first came to Australia.

Following its arrival into Australia, the dingo was readily accepted into Aboriginal life, both practically and spiritually, and became one of the most represented animals in Aboriginal mythology. The dingo was seen as a creator, the ancestor of humans, and on Fraser Island it was considered a protector. Because dingoes lived both in the physical and mystical realms, they were thought to be able to perceive evil spirits undetectable by humans, and therefore made valuable guarders of camp sites.

Dingoes were also seen as the spirits of family members coming back to visit after they had died.

Sometimes dingoes acted as guard dogs – usually against human or spirit intruders – and as bed warmers or 'walking blankets' on cold nights. Dingoes were also useful camp site cleaners and valuable companions. Childless women treated them as child substitutes, and children used dingoes as cute and furry play toys.

The dingo has been part of the life of Indigenous Australians ever since it first appeared in Australia a few thousand years ago.

Ted Evans Collection, Northern Territory Library

The Aborigines took dingo pups from their natal dens and tamed them. They named their dingoes with great affection and if their dingo was harmed, it became an object of great dispute. They patted and caressed their dingoes, groomed them, and tenderly rubbed noses with them, in imitation of the dingo's own manner of greeting and adoration of each other.

Indigenous women nursed dingo pups from their own breasts and also carried dingoes on walkabout, like they carried their own babies and children. When a dingo reached adulthood, it was free to leave the Aboriginal camp for the wild.

Today the Butchulla people – the traditional owners of Fraser Island – still enjoy the company of camp dingoes which remain wild but visit often and enjoy sitting by their campfires at night.

Two elders of the Pintupi people, Lake Mackay, Western Australia, with dingo pups they used for hunting.

9

European arrival

When the First Fleet arrived at Sydney Cove in 1788, with over 1500 men, women and children, it was met by a local Aboriginal tribe, who lived mainly on the harvest of the sea. The local people referred to their wild dog companions as 'dingo', and although other tribes with different languages called it by different names, such as 'warrigal' (or Wangari on Fraser Island), the name dingo stuck, and this is the name we have used ever since.

Soon came the pastoralists with their sheep and other livestock. The new farmers cleared and fenced the land for their introduced farm animals, in an attempt to exclude the large marsupials which competed with their stock for the precious grasses. Dingoes learned to hunt the introduced species, possibly because they were faced with reduced numbers of their favoured prey – large marsupials.

A somewhat fanciful depiction of a dingo from Surgeon John White's 'Journal of a Voyage to New South Wales', 1790.

Private Collection © Oryx Publishing

The colonists took immediate measures to protect their precious stock, which grew as an industry within years. Thus began an era of eradication for Australia's iconic dingo, which has continued through till today.

Within the colony's first 50 years of settlement, a bounty for dingo scalps was implemented – and even today bounties for dingo scalps are still paid in some states of Australia. Dingo scalps became valuable trade for Aboriginal people, made reliant on the new settlers due to the loss of their lands and traditional food sources.

Within the first hundred years of settlement, the poison strychnine was widely in use, causing a significant decline in dingo numbers.

Hidden in the scrub, looking straight at the camera, the eyes of this female seem to be searching for signs of betrayal.

11

Dingoes have made a home on Fraser Island for at least the last 1000 years.

Forced into hiding, the dingo became a secretive and guarded creature, suspicious and wary of humans, as we now know it today. In some areas of the country, trapping, shooting, and poisoning have led to the complete eradication of dingoes.

Despite human persecution the dingo continues to prove itself a worthy adversary, and it is perhaps only its tenacity which has saved it from complete extinction.

The dingo, once friend of the Aboriginal people, was also known to befriend the European invaders.

The greatest threat to the survival of the Fraser Island dingo is humans.

Tourism on Fraser Island relies heavily on the fact that visitors might have a chance to see a dingo in the wild.

A home on Fraser Island

The visitors from around the world who flock to Fraser Island each year are enthralled by the iconic dingo. Tour buses and barges stop their hectic schedules to admire and enjoy the chance to observe our top-end carnivore predator. It is a highlight of any tour when sightseers have the opportunity to observe a 'real Australian dingo', whether up close, or from the window of a tour bus. There is never a dull moment for dingoes who venture out onto the beach.

Supremely versatile, the dingo has a great capacity to adapt to any climate, ecosystem, or territory. It has managed to make itself a home in many parts of Australia, from dense lush rainforest to sparse desert, from snow-covered mountains to dry saltbush plains; from marshy grassland to arid claypans and spinifex.

Are dingoes really aggressive … or just curious? They have no choice but to share their habitat with humans on Fraser Island.

Dingoes seem to have a knack for finding the most beautiful places to live!

The dingo's territory

A pack of dingoes will usually occupy an area of territory bordered by features of the natural landscape. The size of a territory varies depending on the landscape and the abundance of food and water, and is often referred to as a 'home range'. Dingoes spend most of their time resting within a part of their home range called the 'core area' or 'centre of activity'. Core areas have the most protective cover and resources for dingoes to hide and survive. The home range is the overall area that either an individual or family lives in and can cover an area of between 10 and 300 square kilometres. The core area however, is much smaller and may only be five to ten square kilometres in size.

Home ranges for individuals or packs often overlap, to accommodate shared resources such as water holes, but their 'core areas' usually remain separate.

Swamps and lagoons provide ample hunting opportunities for the dingo.

Packs of dingoes that live adjacent to each other try to avoid being in shared areas at the same time in order to minimise potential conflicts with their neighbours. They avoid conflicts by maintaining 'scent posts' – places where they urinate or defecate. They also howl to alert other dingoes of their presence there.

The core area of the dingo's territory is usually out of bounds to strangers. Individuals and packs will strongly defend their territories and core areas against outsiders when they have to.

OPPOSITE: *This dingo is not hunting a goanna – he is attempting to rip my backpack down from its hanging place in the tree!*

Dingoes prefer flight to fight but will defend their territory assertively when necessary.

The dingo has a large head, oversize ears that stand erect, and an elongated muzzle.

What is a dingo?

The dingo is thought to be descended from the small pale coloured wolves, the Indian Wolf or the Arabian Wolf. It is also closely related to the Thai dingo, the New Guinea Singing Dog and the Siberian husky.

Compared to its distant relative the Gray Wolf, the dingo is on average a smallish animal. It stands roughly 57 cm high at the shoulder (the wolf stands up to 95 cm), it is 123 cm long from nose to tail tip (wolves are up to 200 cm long) and it weighs approximately 16–22 kg (the wolf weighs up to 64 kg). Males are usually larger and heavier than females.

Like many canids (members of the dog family), dingoes can adapt quickly to their environment. Those in alpine areas appear to have a thicker coat and carry more weight than those in the desert, although both are the same species.

Most dingoes are ginger in colour, ranging from dark, reddish ochre to light beige. Roughly 17 per cent are black-and-tan, with a tan highlight on the face and legs.

An adult dingo's tail is substantial and feathery, and when held upright, gives the animal a majestic stature.

Regardless of their coat colour, most dingoes have white marks on their feet (often referred to as 'socks') and a white tail tip (which may consist of only a few white hairs). Some dingoes may have a white chest patch and others can have black hairs along their backs that may look similar to the black saddle common to German shepherd dogs.

There are several differences between the dingo and the domestic dog, the most obvious of these is their vocal behaviour – dingoes communicate by howling and only growl when alarmed. Another difference is their breeding cycle – dingoes breed only once a year whereas domestic dogs can breed twice.

Broadly speaking, the dingo has a longer muzzle, larger ears, elongated teeth, and a flatter and larger skull, giving it the overall appearance of having a big head for its body size.

The dark 'guard' hairs on these Fraser Island dingo pups fade with age.

Dingoes don't bark; they communicate by howling.

Fraser Island dingoes usually have one or more white 'socks'.

Tropical, Alpine and Desert are sub-categories of the dingo. Dingoes can be black or white as well as ginger. All have one or more white 'socks' and white tail tips.

Differences in their DNA can be used to differentiate Fraser Island dingoes from domestic captive bred dingoes. In addition, DNA can be used to determine relatedness between groups of wild dingoes.

Dingoes live for approximately five to seven years in the wild, depending on the circumstances – some can live up to 10 years. People who study dingoes refer to a young dingo under six months old as a 'pup', a dingo between six and nine months as a 'juvenile', and a dingo between nine and 20 months as a 'yearling'. A dingo that is 21 months or older is usually referred to as an 'adult'.

Senses on alert!

A dingo's survival depends on its entire sensory system, not only sight, sound and smell, but also such things as taste, touch and balance. Using all of its senses, the dingo is able to hunt, communicate, play and coexist with other dingoes, whether part of its own family, or an outside pack.

A dingo's ability to see detail is a lot poorer than ours because colour and detail are not high priorities for survival. As their prey items are quite often camouflaged, the dingo's capacity to see movement is more important and, combined with their strong sense of smell and hearing, even well-disguised prey items become susceptible to capture.

With its eyes set fairly widely apart, a dingo has an almost 240° field of vision. They can hunt efficiently by day and at night, making good use of their ability to see things in low light levels. Their night vision is enhanced by a large cornea and lens, which allow more light to enter the eye. Dingoes are most active in mornings and afternoons.

Even on the darkest nights, a dingo is able to move around with assurance and poise due to the exceptional light-harvesting ability of its eyes.

25

A dingo can swivel its ears independently in order to pick up sounds coming from different directions.

Like all canids, the dingo has excellent hearing ability. The large outer ear (the pinna) of a dingo pup looks out of proportion to the rest of its body – indeed they do have to 'grow into their ears' eventually, although the dingo's ears always look large and impressive.

The many muscles that control its ear movement, enable a dingo to rotate each ear almost 180° – either simultaneously or independently. When one ear picks up a sound, both ears focus in that direction in order to concentrate the sound waves, allowing the animal to locate the source of the sound quickly and precisely.

OPPOSITE: I called this dingo 'Teakie'. She swivels an ear to perhaps capture the sound of her mate hidden in the bush, while she basks in the sun on the beach.

Out in the open, a dingo can hear the howls of other dingoes many kilometres away, while also being able to detect the soft rustle of movement made by a small mammal or lizard creeping through the undergrowth. The range of sound frequencies that dingoes can hear is far greater than ours, so the dingo can hear pitches that we cannot.

The dingo's sense of smell is many times greater than ours – it may smell something that's two or three kilometres away. A dingo can divert air backwards, away from what it is investigating by exhaling through the openings on the side of the nose. In this way a fresh scent is obtained each time inhalation occurs. Their exceptional sense of smell is perhaps the reason that canids seem to be able to sense 'fear' – they may detect the stress hormones in the sweat – in both people and other dingoes.

A dingo has only a fraction of the number of the taste buds of a human but, like us, its sense of taste and smell are interlinked. Their superior sense of smell seems to dominate their approach to eating, and the need to provide food for themselves is more imperative than the taste of the food.

OPPOSITE: *It might look like it's just having a sniff, but the dingo will be checking for intruders or on the trail of a meal. A dingo can scent us from our footprints.*

A dingo can move each nostril independently to help detect the direction that a scent is coming from. Its nostrils flare to take in more air when it runs.

Like other canids, a dingo has an impressive set of teeth – 42 in all. Its canine teeth are long and narrow, compared to those of a domestic dog, but they become blunt over time. They are designed to tear and shear at the prey, and to wound it rather than cut or stab it.

The incisor teeth at the front of its mouth seize and hold its prey still, with the strength of the jaw causing the crushing finale. Its 'carnassial' teeth (which sit behind the canines) are its butchering equipment, which it uses to remove tissue from the dead prey.

The sharp cutting edges of their incisors work like scissors, confining hide between the two surfaces and slicing through it to reveal the flesh within.

The dingo uses its molars, or rear teeth, for crushing and grinding bone.

OPPOSITE: When dingoes bare their teeth like this it is not necessarily a sign of aggression – it is often part of their play behaviour.

This four-month-old pup is exercising his teeth on a log, demonstrating how strong and capable he is becoming.

When feeling defensive, irritated, threatened, or when making a threat, a dingo raises its hackles – in a display known as 'bristling'.

Living together

Dingoes have many ways of communicating with each other – one of which is body language. A dingo uses its ears, tail, posture and even its fur to let another dingo know how it is feeling.

Ears set back signify submission, fear, or concentration, while ears that are erect tell other dingoes that an individual is comfortable or asserting dominance. A simple twitch of the ear may tell another member of the pack whether its time to play or time to fight.

The tail likewise demonstrates a message. A tail held high and curled over the back signifies the individual is demonstrating confidence or dominance; when the tail is held low or tucked tightly between the legs, it shows apprehension or submission to a parent or older sibling. Positions in between these two extremes suggest either neutrality of status between individuals, or a disposition of relaxation, playfulness, or concentration. A loose, wagging tail indicates wellbeing or contentment.

The body language of these pups tells its own story of their heartbreak over being punished by Dad, having spent so much time waiting for him to return.

Dingo pups are always seeking touch – even adult dingoes seem to like the comforting sensation of a mate close by.

As its tail is a fairly obvious feature of the dingo, other dingoes approaching from a distance are able to identify the mood of the animal they are approaching well in advance.

Like humans, dingoes are tactile animals and appreciate the comfort of touch. Research has found that a canid's heart rate is reduced when it comes into contact with a comforting touch, much like the way our blood pressure is lowered when we pat a dog or get a hug from a friend. They also appreciate having soft things around their bodies to lie on or snuggle up to.

Because the pups are born blind, they are equipped with an even greater sensitivity to touch so that they are able to feel where their mother is. As with most communal living animals, dingoes that have an assertive role over other members of their group are better able to fight disease, tend to grow larger, have increased energy and confidence, and are generally healthier.

A dingo's sensitive whiskers can feel the flutter of a fly's wings.

'Kirra' shows off her ability to climb a two-metre vertical sand bank with ease.

The ability to move quickly and easily through a variety of habitats is important to dingoes. They may have to scale sheer, rocky cliff faces, navigate through harsh, uneven environments, or tunnel through or climb over seemingly impenetrable vegetation.

The dingo's well developed sense of balance, combined with suppleness and flexibility, allow it to stretch, bend, snake and squeeze their bodies through and around obstacles with speed and agility.

Dingoes are very agile animals with great joint elasticity. They are able to alter their path with nimble speed and lightning decision-making. Their physical strength and endurance complement their sharp reflexes, allowing them to handle many difficult situations.

As well as having great strength and flexibility, dingoes have an excellent sense of balance.

A dingo may need all the stamina it can muster when on the hunt.

A key to survival is stamina and endurance – a dingo can walk or trot for lengthy periods over long distances. It may also need plenty of energy and an ability for prolonged exertion when hunting large prey.

An orderly society

Dingoes live in a society governed mostly by the availability of food. They generally have strong family bonds and a strong spirit of affection towards others in their group. They may, however, evict members if resources are insufficient.

Mostly dingoes enjoy lifelong bondings with their mates. They prefer to avoid conflict wherever possible and prefer to engage in friendly greetings and play. These wild, intense, free-spirited and dignified animals appear to live with grace and courage, passion and determination.

A group of dingoes is often known as a 'pack'. The term 'pack' usually refers to a group of dingoes that maintain and defend their territory and hunt cooperatively.

BELOW: '*Old Greg*' *leads his pups on a foray to teach them to explore and hunt, but forays also offer a chance to play together.*

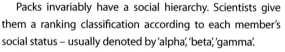

The alpha male or the alpha female usually leads a foray; any lower-ranked pack members travel behind.

Packs invariably have a social hierarchy. Scientists give them a ranking classification according to each member's social status – usually denoted by 'alpha', 'beta', 'gamma'.

The parents are the 'alpha' (dominant) male and female and are typically the only two members of the pack who come from unrelated parents and therefore have genetic differences. Usually the 'alpha' male is dominant over all other members, and the alpha female is dominant over all but the 'alpha' male.

Quite often, the 'alpha' female leads the group when they travel. Alpha pack members appear to initiate activities, make the decisions, and lead the group on forays, deciding when to travel and when to rest. Alpha males and females are usually monogamous although there are exceptions.

The previous year's pups, as well as any adopted members of the group, are often referred to as the 'beta' (second-in-charge) members. They sometimes take on the role of 'helpers' when raising litters of new pups. The remaining siblings and affiliates, plus new or current year's pups are ranked as 'gamma' members. They are subordinate to the older pack members.

The most important role of the pack hierarchy is to maintain stability in the group so they have a united front to defend their core area against intruders and to ensure that the younger members will inherit the territory when the dominant pair die.

The pack congregates to maintain its social bonds, for camaraderie and play, to sleep, to share information, to patrol their boundaries and to share food.

Mum rests while the pups take turns at the food (turtle carcass) and play.

The greeting ceremony

An engaging aspect of dingo behaviour is the greeting ceremony. Even if they have only been separated for a half hour, dingoes greet each other affectionately, as though they haven't seen each other for days. To display their pleasure at the reunion dingoes run around together, wag their tails, touch noses, and lick and mouth each other's muzzles. Scientists believe that wild dogs, including wolves, dingoes and coyotes identify each other by licking and smelling each other's mouth.

Greetings strengthen social bonds, reinforcing group unity. They may also convey information such as where the individual has been, what it has encountered during the expedition, and what it has eaten or rolled in.

Dingoes greet each other affectionately every time they meet; touching and affection dominate their society.

Frequent contact with fellow pack members is part of dingo socitety.

Licking each other can be a form of research – perhaps finding out what someone else has eaten. A pup often licks a parent's face, begging for regurgitation. This is also a sign of submission, as well as a display of affection. Greetings, licking, touching and snuggling are a big part of a dingo's social behaviour – close contact seems to be a way of life.

Maintaining the peace

Fighting among dingoes in a pack is rare and usually avoided with the polite use of submissive behaviours which preserve social harmony within the group. Two types of submission are used – active and passive. 'Active' submissive postures are imitations of the signals pups use to solicit food from their parents. They include: lowering the head and inclining it forwards, attempted face licking; lowering the tail, tucking it between the legs, or wagging it at half mast; pushing the ears back; and crouching the body and perhaps even crawling slowly towards the more dominant dingo. Active submission may also involve giving up food, sitting quietly at a distance and waiting for a turn at eating, or 'licking up' to a more dominant parent or sibling during the greeting ceremony.

Mounting another dingo is a sign of attempted dominance.

An intruder is asking permission to enter the territory. After following certain rituals she was granted passage and allowed to continue on her way.

'Passive' submission is used primarily to prevent a fight or avert escalating aggression during a mild-scale attack. The defensive individual wishing to placate the aggressor rolls on the ground and takes an indefensible position that displays its vulnerable stomach area, with its front paws folded. The dominant animal may stand over it and investigate the exposed stomach and if appeased, the challenge is ended and they both walk away.

The social hierarchy of the group remains mostly stable throughout the year, except for breeding season when dispersing yearlings or lone dingoes become excitable and try to assert some dominance over another in the hope of mating. Usually, dingoes try to limit the need for a fight and try to avoid it with submissive postures. However if a dingo decides not to submit, then a challenge becomes serious and can even escalate into a fight to the death.

A year-old dingo approaches her father submissively.

This young dingo is tired of waiting for a turn at the food and is asserting dominance over its sibling.

In a dominance test the opponents circle for a time, assessing each other. In this case, a display of power began as each dingo tried to prove it could bite higher along the tree branch than the other. Comedy ceased as the real battle began. Surprisingly, the beta male won and the former alpha retired tail between his legs.

With its strong jaws and sharp teeth and claws, a dingo can inflict horrific injuries on its opponent. Most adult dingoes carry the scars of the battle to survive and be 'top dog'.

This alpha male seems to be saying: 'don't mess with my bitch'.

A young bonded pair share a moment of affection.

Raising a family

The alpha pair tend to mate for life and breed each season. Partners will most commonly be found together throughout the year and the mates often show affection towards each other.

Yearlings that have left the safety of the family pack and dispersed to find their own territory need to find a mate. Males are capable of siring pups at twelve months of age, but more typically breed the following season. To prevent inbreeding, lone dingoes must search out a mate from a different pack. Howling increases during the mating season, and howls can be heard far and wide.

Dingoes mate only once a year, mostly during autumn (March–May) so that the pups are whelped in winter (June–August). Alpha females come into oestrus before other females in the pack. Usually females have their first litters at two years of age or older.

Bonded dingoes show affection to each other throughout the year as well as during mating season.

TOP: *Kirra's father Solomon keeps a close watch over Kirra while she is pregnant.*
BOTTOM LEFT: *Kirra at 46 days.*
BOTTOM RIGHT: *Kirra at 57 days.*

As the female's oestrus cycle approaches the dingo pair demonstrate increasing affection for each other; muzzle and genital licking, grooming each other, playing and travelling their home range together, dual scent marking, and sleeping in close companionship. Males scent-mark over the urine of their female partner, to advertise that she has been 'taken' and is not available for mating with another dingo. However, sometimes the couple may be required to fight off approaches from other potential mates.

Choosing a den in which to give birth seems to be up to the female and her specific needs. Dens are fairly similar despite the varied landscapes that dingoes inhabit.

In central Australia, dingoes take advantage of unused rabbit warrens or wombat holes, while in alpine areas dingoes may choose to dig a den under the roots of large trees or beneath hollow logs; they may also use caves, or burrow under overhanging ledges of rock.

Dens are nearly always close to a water source; some may face a particular direction to take advantage of the sun or to shelter from prevailing winds. Having an elevated den gives some protection against predators.

BOTTOM: *The natal den, two-thirds of the way up a steep hill, provides a good vantage point to the valley below.*
INSET: *This site, also two-thirds of the way up a hill, allows for surveillance of the valley, but has more room. The flattened hilltop above allows a safe place for pups to play as they gain their sight and learn to stretch their legs.*

Kirra's pups roughly knead her tummy while feeding.

These pups are 10 days old and have just opened their eyes; they are wobbly on their feet but are already managing to move around.

After about 63 days of gestation, the female dingo gives birth. Her litter size varies between two to nine pups, but the average litter size is five. At birth the pups weigh between 200 and 300 grams, and are born fairly dark in colour but do have white markings. They are unable to see or hear, and rely on smell and touch to move around, communicating with their mother using whimpers and squeals. The mother licks the pups' genital region to stimulate reflexive urination and defecation, at the same time cleaning them.

At around 10 days old they can support themselves on their forelegs, and their hind legs can support their weight at around 15 days. Other family members tend to stay away from the den area, other than to provide for the mother by delivering a carcass or regurgitating food for her.

As the pups grow they are able to nurse while Kirra stands up.

Cooperative nurturing

The natal den is only used for a week or two, until the pups are able to see, at which time their mother typically moves the pups to a larger den. She continues to nurse them, but leaves a baby sitter with them so she can go out hunting on her own.

Often other members of the dingo group provide care for the new pups. Usually it is the 'beta' members of the pack that give some help. They deliver food for the pups and mother, and guard pups when the parents are away from the den area. These 'alloparental' helpers take their task very seriously. They look after the young as though they were their own offspring and, in some cases, they may delay their own departure to stay and mind their new siblings.

The beta female of the pack, whom I named 'Darling Girl' is baby-sitting a pup.

At three weeks of age, the pups are capable of eating solid food, and the parents bring carcasses to them, as well as regurgitating food and water for them.

From four weeks of age the pups are capable of venturing out of the den. Sometimes the mother will move them to another site . She chooses a place that provides shade and concealment, incorporating a play area and room for them to begin to extend their boundaries. Adult pack members hunt at a distance from this area, allowing the pups to obtain food close by, thus learning hunting and survival skills through game playing and imitation.

The 'rendezvous site' may change every few days, or remain stable according to circumstances. If a perceived threat occurs, or as food sources for pups to forage diminish, the site is changed. The parent achieves this by depositing a carcass for the pups at the new location. Pups follow her to the carcass, and subsequently understand that this is their new rendezvous site.

Paternal care of the young pups is very important. Fathers provide food, protect the natal den, and act as a baby-sitter while the mother dingo goes out hunting.

As well as continuing to nurse, the mother dingo and the helpers regurgitate food for the pups. This usually continues until they are about four months old, although some dingoes on Fraser Island regurgitate for their pups until they are six months old.

At this time the pups are considered weaned, although they will be somewhat dependent on their parents for a few more months. They are taught social skills, the rules of dingo society and communication, and they are allowed to accompany adults on hunting forays, to learn how to search out prey and subsist on their own in their big new world. As the pups grow and are able to embark on their own forays, the pack maintains regular rendezvous sites, and always returns to these sites during the course of the day.

After the age of nine months, a juvenile dingo is usually capable of living on its own. It will either stay with its family group, or it may head out on its own to find a vacant territory to inhabit.

Pups wait longingly for their parents to return with some food and companionship.

This father dingo is reprimanding his daughter. She exhibits submissive body language; her rear low to the ground, tail down, ears back, and attempts to lick his face.

An affectionate father dingo nurtures and grooms the pups, and seems to tolerate them climbing and jumping all over him. However, teaching them survival and social skills is also part of his responsibility.

Dingoes at play

Dingoes seem to delight in all manner of play throughout the day, spontaneously and enthusiastically. Play is not just a way of getting rid of excess energy – it can also serve as practice for later life, improving the animal's coordination and motor skills.

Dingo play might include jaw sparring, high wrestling (both dingoes up on their hind legs, hugging each other while mouthing their opponent), low wrestling (holding each other in a hug on the ground while kicking or biting each other), nose jabbing, shouldering each other, slamming bodies, or 'hide and seek' around objects.

The most common invitation to play is the 'play bow'; the dingo drops its forequarters to the ground while its hindquarters stay up in the air, with tail wagging. This is sometimes accompanied by howling or an open-mouthed 'grin'. On other occasions, a dingo solicits play by rushing at a prospective playmate and pushing them over.

Dingoes show off their agility with graceful and contortionistic play manoeuvres.

Tug-of-war is another of their favourite games. Pups find a particular object which takes on a special significance – be it a pandanus frond or a piece of stolen human property - and shake the object around inviting the others to steal it. A tug-of-war ensues and often precedes a lively and energetic game of 'chasey' that can last 20 minutes as golden bodies charge around the bush at high speed in single file.

In some cases, play caught on camera appears violent and aggressive, however dingoes know their own strength and know how hard to bite before inflicting a wound; their biting during play fighting is almost always inhibited.

On Fraser Island, play can be very boisterous and is often misconstrued as aggression.

While learning to hunt, pups prey on small lizards, grasshoppers, spiders and crabs.

This dingo is feeding on a washed-up turtle carcass.

On the hunt

Dingoes are active during both the day and the night, although they seem to prefer dawn and dusk. Their resourcefulness and versatile activity pattern gives them a wide range of food sources to choose from.

When pups are old enough, the pack hunts larger game together, such as a kangaroo or a wallaby. Cooperative hunting means that a dingo pack can limit the movement of their prey and attack from numerous angles, thus increasing the chance of success. Once the hunt is complete, the dingoes share the kill.

A hunting dingo may use a variety of methods including ambush, stalking and tracking, charging, circling and air scenting, foraging, digging or pouncing – depending on the intended prey. A dingo will also eat carrion which, on Fraser Island, may include a washed up dolphin, dugong or turtle. In outback Australia, one rabbit per day will sustain an adult dingo.

Despite the dingo's reputation as a calculating and relentless predator of livestock, cattle and sheep do not make up a significant percentage of their diet, even in areas where livestock is readily available. On the Australian mainland, foxes and feral cats – which have been implicated in the decline of many small native species – are preyed on by dingoes. So the dingo may, in fact, be doing us a good turn by helping to save some of our indigenous species from extinction.

Although the dingo certainly has a preference for fresh meat, in lean times it will resort to vegetation to supplement its diet. During the spring/summer seasons on Fraser Island, when pups are becoming independent and learning to hunt on their own, they spend a great deal of time eating wild berries that grow on the sand dunes. The berries must make up a fair proportion of their diet at this stage, as their scats are sloppy and blue.

At four months of age the pups still rely heavily on Mum for food. Here 'Princess' hurries into the rendezvous site to regurgitate food for them.

On Fraser Island the dingo's diet consists of bandicoot, echidna, goanna, snake, antechinus, fish, carrion, berries and fruit such as pandanus, mango, and coconut.

Food and feeding

Among the carnivores, it is only members of the canid family that feed their offspring by regurgitation – an ingenious method of bringing pre-digested food to the growing pups.

The alpha female is extremely vulnerable at this time. Letting her defences down, she allows the pups to lick her face, which stimulates a reflex response in the body, resulting in her stomach contents issuing forth back into her oesophagus and mouth. The mother may regurgitate up to three times at each occasion, and in doing so will bring up roughly a third of the food she has eaten. It is a very private moment between a parent and her pups, which prefer regurgitated food to a raw carcass. It is the most exciting time of day for the dependent pups.

Pack social structure is reinforced at feeding times. A pup will often happily share a meal, but occasionally asserts its dominance with a scuffle, forcing weaker members out of the way. Thus the strong survive, and the weak grow weaker and sometimes perish from starvation.

Licking Mum's mouth is not only a way to show affection but also to ask for food.

This pup named 'Mintie' is nearly six months old, but his mother is still providing him with regurgitated food.

Lesser ranked members wishing to share food approach the feeder politely with submissive behaviour. If the pup feeding wants to share, it will admit the approaching pup. Otherwise, the feeder growls and bares a portion of its teeth. The approaching pup sits back and waits patiently and politely until the other has finished eating. Even though a dominant individual is not actually eating the food, he may rush at a sibling who attempts to come anywhere near it.

Anything becomes a potential prey item for growing pups. It may be an echidna, a small lizard, a crab or a small marsupial. Anything that moves will be chased. What begins as a game, may end up as a tasty reward. One of their most endearing traits when detecting prey in tall grass or low-lying scrub is leaping up on their hind legs and landing with stiffened fore legs on their prey. As a follow-through, if the prey is not caught, the pup thrusts its nose into the scrub and 'digs' around for it.

Sharing food is tough for hungry dingo pups – especially when it's only an echidna skin. The pups use the spines as teething rusks.

Meeting, sleeping and cooling off

Dingoes use a variety of settings for their daily rendezvous sites. Usually there is a nice shady tree nearby where pups (and adults) can shelter from the sun, or even from the rain. After all their feeding and play pups need a regular time-out, and 'nap trees' provide safety and security for them.

Generally dingoes sleep wherever they are comfortable. A sleep can last anything from 10 minutes to a few hours, depending on the conditions of the day. When raising pups, adult dingoes return to their rendezvous sites regularly and take a nap with the pups after feeding them. If dingoes are in company they often curl up together, even on hot days, where at least one part of their body will always be touching part of another individual.

Rendezvous sties are safe areas where adult dingoes leave their pups while they go out hunting.

Dingoes are capable of adapting easily to climatic extremes, but like most mammals, if they get too hot they need to cool themselves. As the dingo's temperature rises, its brain stimulates a reflex which increases the respiration rate, and panting begins. Water in the nose, mouth and lungs evaporates, thus cooling the blood.

As well as panting, dingoes use a variety of other methods to cool off. Digging a bed in the ground reveals the cooler earth below the hot surface. Stretching out their bodies complements the cooling effect of a breeze. Sitting under a shady tree, or sitting in water if they have access to it, seems to be their favourite approach.

During winter, the dingo's coat thickens up, with the fur working as insulation against the cold weather and helping to repel water. When the dingo gets too wet and cold though, the response is usually to dig a dry hole under the shelter of a tree, curl up into a tight ball with its nose tucked under its tail as close to a family member as possible to exchange heat and take turns to lick each other dry.

Fraser Island dingoes love the water – especially in summer. The current management practice of scaring them off the beach deprives them of this relief.

Leaving home

Once they mature and become more independent, some pups stay with their natal pack, while others disperse to new areas. We don't really know how these decisions to stay or go are made. It may be an advantage for the breeding pair to retain as many of their yearling pups as possible to help raise subsequent litters, instead of forcing them to leave. On the other hand, if there is a shortage of prey within the home range, the area may be unable to sustain an increase in pack size.

Alteration of the status of pack members owing to tension or disruption of their social hierarchy through human interference – such as shooting or trapping – may also contribute to dispersal. Aerial baiting campaigns can wipe out entire packs, leaving vacant territories for new dingoes to inhabit.

As the pups grow older, decisions have to be made as to whether they stay with the family group or leave to start their own pack.

Very little is known about why and when dingoes disperse. Sometimes a small group of dingoes will leave the natal pack and re-form as a satellite pack in a different area of the home range. Ultimately, successful dispersal depends on the availability of vacant areas in which to settle, or incorporation into a different, existing social unit.

A dingo that leaves its natal pack at too young an age faces an uncertain future.

On Fraser Island, a dingo as young as ten months may begin to leave the pack. The process of dispersal begins with the individual spending more time apart from its natal pack, embarking on investigative forays out of the home range in an attempt to find a vacant territory. Over a period of time the individual slowly dissociates from members of the pack, until it is eventually ready to leave.

A dingo that stays with its parents for 12 months is more likely to survive than those which become independent at a younger age. More time spent with adults means more time learning to hunt effectively. The young dingo also gains the advantage of group hunting by staying with its pack.

Call of the wild

There is nothing quite as captivating as the melancholy howl of a dingo when alone in the Australian bush. Suddenly, you are not alone any longer. You wonder: is a pup crying for his parent to return? Is a female searching for her mate? Are they calling all reserves together to defend their territory? Or is a hunt about to take place?

Howling may sound fairly 'uniform' to us, but each individual has its own voice, and the diverse tones and sounds all have a meaning. A dingo's howl may have many parts – sometimes a steady note, sometimes changing notes, or an abrupt short yelp.

Most researchers believe that howling is a long-range communication technique that helps locate other members of the pack, or to warn trespassers. By howling the various members of the family can stay in touch during hunting forays, announce their presence at a rendezvous point or shared locality, ward off entry by trespassing dingoes, or let others know that they are about to move.

'Lightning' learns to find her voice, but her howls are high pitched and feeble. She won't start yodeling for another few months!

Howling may also be used to attract a mate, and to alert pups to danger or invite them for a feed. Pups howl for their parents to return, or if they are lost. A parent responds to let the pup know they are on their way to help. Pup howls are distinctive because of their high pitch and tentative qualities, as they learn to find their own voice.

Chorus howls look as impressive as they sound. The dingo's whole body seems to be involved in the process of howling.

Counterpoint howls occur when a lone howl is heard by other members of a pack and they in turn respond. This sometimes becomes a chorus. When a chorus howl is performed, nearby dingoes who are listening are able to determine how many members of the pack are in close proximity from each different voice. Group howling may also serve to unify and bolster the relationships within a social unit.

As well as howling, dingoes growl and moan; shorter-range communications that are not as loud as their distinctive, plaintive trademark. If danger presents itself, a dingo may bark-howl; the bark is shorter and more recognisable as a cough, followed by a lingering howl.

Fraser Island dingoes howl at passing aircraft.

One of their most endearing characteristics is the 'snuff', a response they use when they are startled or alarmed, but sometimes just inquisitive. Similar to a sneeze the snuff is a quick exhalation of air which despite its low intensity can be heard by other pack members at short distances, and is sometimes accompanied by a delightful little shake of the head.

On Fraser Island, dingoes also have the curious habit of howling at the light aircraft which traverse the Island. Nearly every one of the 57 individuals I have observed over seven years on the island has howled at a plane. However the screaming sound of a passing F1-11 army jet – while deafening and upsetting to the human ear – does not usually inspire a vocal response from the dingoes.

Because dingoes can track each other down precisely after hours of separation, it may appear that they have some sort of psychic communication ability. However, it is not telepathy, but by the use of a clever network of 'scent posts'.

'Scent rolling' is a form of communication.

A scent post is an accessible prominent item such as a tree or shrub located at the intersection of shared territories. The dingo marks the scent post with urine, faeces or a pheromone secretion. A scent posts is sometimes 'raked' by the individual to bring extra attention to it, leaving additional pheromones from the scent glands in its foot pads. Scent posts are ingenious methods of marking paths for friends to follow or foes to stay away from.

Their outstanding sense of smell gives the dingo the ability to decipher each scent. Dingoes are able to discriminate between layers of scents, even if a stronger smell has been placed over the existing one. We can only guess at the information that these posts contain – they form a vital part of each dingo's communication network.

Raised leg urination seems to be performed only by the alpha male (and female in a squat with raised leg), whereas lesser ranked males usually squat to urinate.

'Old Greg' and 'Princess' return to their den after a hunting trip.

Battle scarred and bristling, this huge alpha male strikes an imposing figure as he stalks through the bush in search of prey. Parks rangers tag the dingoes in order to keep track of them.

Observing dingoes in the wild

Researchers use tracking collars, scent baits, or thermal imaging technology to locate dingoes in the wild. Without these aids, often the only way of finding them – apart from hearing them howl – is the small clue of the temporary footprint left behind in the sand.

Their brief passing through a certain place in a convoy inevitably leaves paw print trails and eventually, after some time, carves a semi-permanent imprint onto the landscape. Following these trails to an active rendezvous site is no mean feat – dingoes can sometimes make phony routes just in case they are pursued.

The reward once a genuine trail is followed is to find a dingo pad that is fresh. Scratchings in the dirt and smoothed beds – usually under shade trees – are signs that the area is still used.

'Mango' with a GPS tracking collar fitted by researchers from Griffith University.

Protecting the dingo

The dingo is listed as a vulnerable species by the International Union for the Conservation of Nature (IUCN). However, on the Australian mainland, continued hybridisation with domestic dogs may lead to the extinction of dingoes. Poison baiting and control programs pose an even greater threat.

World Heritage listed Fraser Island provides a critical sanctuary for the dingo. It is one of the few remaining places where dingoes may be easily observed in the wild and the Island provides the best chance of preserving the species. However, persecution by humans is now threatening the very survival of the Fraser Island dingo. Over the last several years more than 100 animals which exhibited so-called 'agressive' behaviour have been killed.

Although dingoes have enjoyed human companionship for thousands of years, spending time with dingoes on

Fraser Island is one of the few places where you can see dingoes in the wild.

Fraser island is now discouraged. While adult dingoes tend to stay in the bush, juvenile animals enjoy their time at play and are curious about each new group of humans that inhabits their territory. The boisterous approaches of young dingoes can easily be misconstrued as attack behaviour.

Most dingoes on the Island are tagged so that each animal is easily identifiable. If a park ranger sees a particular dingo interacting with people on too many occasions it becomes classified as a 'problem animal' and will most likely be destroyed.

So for the sake of the dingoes on Fraser Island, enjoy seeing them in the wild, take as many photos as you like, but don't encourage them to come near you or your vehicle. We want Fraser Island dingoes to survive for many generations so others who come to see dingoes in the wild can enjoy them as well.

The dingoes of Fraser Island are disappearing fast. The way you behave towards them is important in helping to protect them.

Acknowledgements

It is with gratitude that I acknowledge just some of my Butchulla friends who have helped me over the years: Aunty Marie, Aunty Francis, Aunty Mallee, Aunty Rossie, Aunty Lillian, Aunty Joyce, Uncle George, Uncle Joe, Nick, Smiley, Sam, Daniel, Travis, Neville (Pie) Navo, Debbra, Paula, Hayden, Dyneale, Opal, and also Uncle Alex and Aunty Eve, Gubi Gubi elders from Brisbane.

I would also like to extend my appreciation to the Save Fraser Island Dingoes (SFID) committee and members, and affiliated organisations for their dedication to saving the dingo. Great appreciation to Fraser Explorer Barges for courtesy vehicle transport to the Island. Deepest love and gratitude to my family and personal friends for believing in my dream. And thanks to Nick Alexander for his hard work and dedication in making this book a beautiful reality.

Produced under
permit from the
Queensland Parks
and Wildlife Service

Queensland
Government